IMAGES
of America

McClellan Air Force Base

I0792621

Civilian police controlled the thousands of automobiles that entered McClellan Air Force Base every day during the 1960s.

ON THE COVER: The first mass meeting at McClellan occurred at the peak of World War II. Gen. Clinton Howard called upon all personnel, civilian and military, of McClellan to discuss the war effort that McClellan would be providing. The military and civilian personnel at McClellan were essentially the pioneers of the base. They would be responsible for expanding the infrastructure of McClellan, increasing their capacity to supply the military with supplies and aircraft throughout World War II. (Courtesy McClellan Museum archives.)

IMAGES
of America

McCLELLAN AIR FORCE BASE

Kyle Byard and Tom Naiman

ARCADIA
PUBLISHING

ISBN 978-0-7385-4762-6

Published by Arcadia Publishing
Charleston, South Carolina

Printed in the United States of America

Library of Congress Catalog Card Number: 2007921335

For all general information contact Arcadia Publishing at:
Telephone 843-853-2070
Fax 843-853-0044
E-mail sales@arcadiapublishing.com
For customer service and orders:
Toll-Free 1-888-313-2665

Visit us on the Internet at www.arcadiapublishing.com

ACKNOWLEDGMENTS

We wish to thank the McClellan Museum archives and Linda Geissinger for the use of these historic photographs showing the base's journey from its construction in 1936 to its closure in 2001 and beyond.

CONTENTS

FOREWORD

Those who lived, worked and played at McClellan's installation did so with professionalism and pride, with integrity and insight, and with enthusiasm and efficiency—traits required to support so many diverse aircraft, communication, munitions, missile, command and control, and logistics systems. From prop to jet aircraft, from grenades to nukes, from radios to satellite control systems, McClellan's workforce continually adapted and painstakingly trained so it could restore and improve the tools used by our armed forces around the globe. Difficult repairs required around the world at a moment's notice were routinely supported by the quiet warrior workforce of McClellan.

The dedicated civilian and military men and women who worked, lived, and served at the installation that would finally be named McClellan Air Force Base (AFB) can be justifiably proud of their contributions to the Army Air Corps, the United States Air Force, the Department of Defense and the nation. From 1938 through 2001, they maintained, repaired, improved, and modernized weapon systems that helped the United States win wars, positively shape world events, and build the greatest military force in the history of the world.

Perhaps no greater task was asked of the McClellan workforce than to simultaneously support the air war over Serbia, close down their installation, and train others that would eventually replace them at other air force bases—they did that with the same professionalism and honor that marked all their previous work. For their accomplishments, we the United States owe them greatly.

Protecting America's security and overseas interests were not the only attributes the employees of McClellan provided. The Sacramento community received numerous activities of charity from the enthusiastic McClellan workforce.

This book commemorates McClellan's entire workforce, from those that moved their families from Rockwell Air Depot in San Diego in 1936 and helped build McClellan to those families that helped close McClellan Air Force Base in 2001.

–Mike Wiedemer
Major General USAF (Retired)
SM-ALC's (McClellan Air Force Bases) last commander

INTRODUCTION

On September 8, 1936, California governor F. F. Merriam presided over the ceremonial groundbreaking of the Pacific Air Depot, which would eventually become known as McClellan Air Force Base. Over the next three years, workers from the Rockwell Air Depot in San Diego built the new facility and transferred operations from the facility at North Island. The initial cost to construct the Sacramento Air Depot was $7 million. The depot began operating early in 1939, and the base was officially dedicated on April 29, 1939. The dedication ceremony turned out over 50,000 curious local residents. On December 1, 1939, Sacramento Air Depot was renamed after the aviation pioneer Maj. Hezekiah "Hez" McClellan, who died tragically while flight-testing a Consolidated PB-2A in May 1936.

When the Empire of Japan bombed Pearl Harbor On December 7, 1941, the mobilization for World War II swept over McClellan. By 1943, McClellan Army Airfield's workforce had increased from the original 357 Rockwell workers to nearly 22,000 military and civilian personnel. When the air force separated from the army and became a separate service in September 1947, McClellan Field was renamed McClellan Air Force Base (AFB) and became an international supply and repair center. The growth of McClellan AFB created thousands of jobs in Sacramento, maintaining the U.S. Air Force through World War II, the Korean War, Vietnam, the cold war, Desert Storm, and the air war over Serbia. Although most aircraft would fly to their destination from McClellan, aircraft and equipment would also be packaged and shipped from McClellan to the Sacramento River Docks, where large barges would take them down the Sacramento to Alameda for shipment overseas. Literally tens of thousand of aircraft passed through McClellan AFB during its years of service.

McClellan's workforce of skilled technicians serviced, overhauled, or retrofitted over 85 different types of bombers, fighters, refueling aircraft, weather reconnaissance aircraft, trainers, and cargo transports. In 1967, during the Vietnam War, McClellan experienced its highest total population of 26,326 military and civilian workers. From that high point until its closure in 2001, McClellan's civilian and military workforce held steady at nearly 18,000 people.

McClellan AFB expanded almost continuously over the years, eventually filling nearly 3,000 acres with over 100 maintenance buildings and 200 shops, totaling over 3 million square feet of space. McClellan AFB was a small city that supported both working and residential communities. Services such as the barbershops, dental clinic, hospital, base exchange, commissary, pizza parlor, bowling alley, movie theater, gymnasium, chapel, library, childcare facility, dining halls, airman and officer clubs, and housing were all provided within walking distance of each other. Over the years, McClellan expanded beyond its main installation and maintained satellite facilities in Lincoln and Davis, Camp Kohler, and the Sacramento River Docks. Over and over again, McClellan outgrew itself and needed to add new housing and support facilities.

Although the base has been closed since 2001, most of the old McClellan buildings survive and have been remodeled for civilian use. The hospital, base exchange, and commissary continue to serve the Sacramento military community. On any given day, the parking lots at these facilities are packed with vehicles of veteran and current military personnel. The U.S. Coast Guard, which moved a fleet of planes to McClellan in September 1978, still actively operates out of the base and continues to conduct search-and-rescue missions along the Pacific Coast year-round.

Throughout its 63 years of existence, McClellan AFB employed tens of thousands of civilian and military employees, many of whom spent their entire professional careers there.

From the original $7 million that was allocated by the U.S. War Department to construct the Pacific Air Depot, McClellan AFB grew into a multi-billion-dollar facility with a global reach of services. In 1995, following the end of the cold war, the Base Realignment and Closure Commission announced that McClellan AFB's workload would be transferred to other air force bases around the country. McClellan officially closed its gates on July 13, 2001.

One

A Modern Base

Following the end of World War I, the Army Air Corps demobilized, scrapping aircraft and closing bases. One casualty of this draw down was the closure of Mather Army Air Field in Sacramento, which had an immediate negative economic impact on the area.

In response to the loss of Mather Field, Arthur S. Dudley, manager of the Sacramento Chamber of Commerce, launched an assault on Congress and the War Department to get it reopened. Dudley testified several times before congressional committees, joined forces with representatives from other regions who were also seeking defense projects, and found willing allies in the army leadership, who saw the need for a major West Coast air base to fight the Pacific war they feared was imminent.

Four years of intense political lobbying and public relations work by Dudley and others led to Pres. Franklin Roosevelt authorizing the construction of six new air bases when he signed the Wilcox Act into law on August 12, 1935. Dudley's efforts had all been aimed at reopening Mather Field, but once the law was passed, army general Oscar Westover presented him with a surprising choice. Westover told Dudley that he could either have Mather Field reopened or have Sacramento be the site for a West Coast repair depot. Realizing both the economic benefits of a repair base and the likelihood that Mather would be reopened anyway, Dudley chose the repair base.

Sacramento was ideally suited for a repair base. It was centrally located along the West Coast, had good flying weather year-round, and was far enough inland that it was safe from a naval assault. A flurry of sometimes dubious land deals obtained nearly 1,100 acres of marginal farmland northeast of Sacramento, and army major John Austin designed an initial layout for the facility in time for California governor F. F. Merriam to perform the ceremonial ground-breaking in September 1936.

Over the next three years, the Sacramento Air Depot was built from tons of concrete brought in by truck and railcar from all over California at a cost of $3 million. The depot was a new type of army base. Unlike the existing Army Air Corps fields, this base was not a modified cavalry post. It would have no stables or parade field. The new depot was designed around long runways, large hangars, and industrial repair shops. It was built for the air age and would grow with military aviation.

Arthur M. Dudley surveys the future site of the Sacramento Air Depot in 1936. The property was vacant grassland northeast of Sacramento and used mostly for grazing cattle.

California governor Frank F. Merriam detonates a ceremonial first charge of dynamite to begin the construction of the Sacramento Air Depot on September 8, 1936. Maj. Arthur Parker of the Quartermaster Corps holds a shovel made from an aircraft propeller at his side.

The ground-breaking ceremony took place on September 8, 1936. Dignitaries included Arthur S. Dudley, Brig. Gen. Delois Emmons, Congressman Frank Buck, California governor Frank Merriam, Maj. Gen. George Simonds, and Brig. Gen. Henry Arnold.

A survey crew places stakes for the airfield construction in 1936. Erected on open agricultural land northeast of Sacramento, the Sacramento Air Depot was one of the first Army Air Corps installations built specifically for air operations rather than as a modified infantry or calvary post.

This is the Sacramento Air Depot's first Headquarters Building. This farmhouse was the temporary office of the constructing quartermaster. It remained in use after the depot opened and was not demolished until 1970.

Engineers review the plans for the Base Headquarters Building in 1937. Major Parker oversaw every detail of construction personally until he was injured in an automobile accident in June 1937. He died during the siege of Battaan in the Philippines in World War II.

The foundations of the maintenance hangar and supply building were excavated in September 1937. The Headquarters Building, hospital, post exchange, and firehouse are well under way to the right.

The steel skeleton of the maintenance hangar rises next to the water tower. The tower was the first structure built at the Sacramento Air Depot.

Engineers inspect the construction of the maintenance hangar's steel framework in 1937. One worker, David Thompson, was killed when he fell from the rafters of Hangar 51. He was the only person killed during the three years of construction.

This photograph shows the maintenance hangar interior in 1938. The huge maintenance bays were designed to service more than 30 aircraft at a time.

This shows early steel-and-concrete framing of the post exchange in 1937. The facade of the exchange included ornate relief sculptures and art deco touches around the main entry.

The post exchange nears completion in 1938. Centrally located between the officers' houses, Headquarters Building, and the enlisted barracks, the spacious exchange was designed to have everything a soldier and his family would ever need under one roof.

This photograph shows early construction of the firehouse and guardhouse near Gate One in 1937.

Here is the finished firehouse in 1939. The Sacramento Air Depot boasted one of the most modern and well-equipped fire departments in California. It frequently responded to emergencies around the Sacramento area.

Gate One was the primary entry to McClellan, connecting the base with Watt Avenue. The firehouse can be seen on the right and the main repair hangar on the left.

Gate Two was the ceremonial entrance to the base. It took important visitors the length of the landscaped mall, past the officers club and housing, directly to the Headquarters Building. The gate was closed in 1960 and removed in 1977.

Here construction begins on the officers' housing area in 1937. The houses were built in white concrete; a distinctly "California" style instead of the wood and brick used at Eastern and Midwestern army posts.

This photograph shows construction of the officers' housing in 1938. All of the buildings were cast concrete with faux brick facades. Officer housing surrounded the McClellan Mall and the officers club.

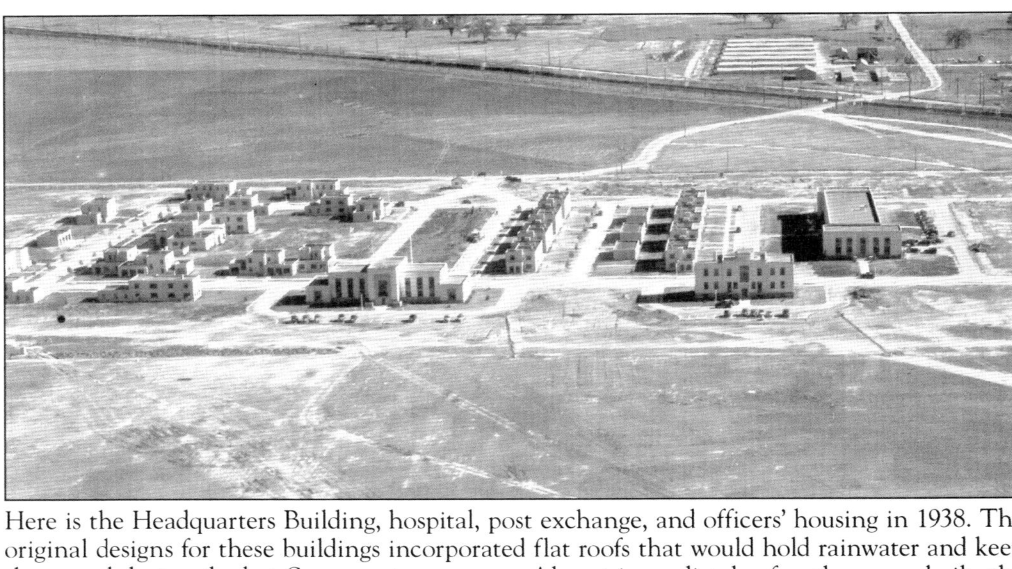

Here is the Headquarters Building, hospital, post exchange, and officers' housing in 1938. The original designs for these buildings incorporated flat roofs that would hold rainwater and keep them cool during the hot Sacramento summers. Almost immediately after they were built, the ceilings began to leak, and the roofs were redesigned to allow water to drain off.

Maj. Arthur Parker of the Army Quartermaster Corps surveys the nearly completed officers' housing from the roof of the Headquarters Building in 1939.

This photograph shows the officers' quarters and post hospital at the opening of the Sacramento Air Depot in 1939. The expansion of the depot during World War II accelerated the planned housing supply, and new housing was constructed across Watt Avenue. The entire officer housing area quickly became a neighborhood for senior officers and non-commissioned officers.

Here are the post hospital, Headquarters Building, and McClellan Mall near completion in 1938. The farmland across Watt Avenue from the post hospital quickly developed to support the expanding depot.

Here is the McClellan water tower between Maintenance Hangar 251 and the supply building (Building 250) in 1938.

The post hospital is under construction in 1937. The capacity of the main facility was quickly overwhelmed, and a string of temporary buildings, connected by wooden walkways, sprung up behind it.

Troops practice for the Dedication Day ceremonies in April 1939. Heavy rains turned the parade field into a swamp, forcing them to move their marching and drill practice onto the paved streets.

Freshly paved taxiways lead to the newly painted hangar on the eve of Dedication Day in April 1939.

Aircraft fill the depot's parking ramp even before construction of the maintenance hangars is complete. Almost every type of aircraft in the Army Air Corps was on display at McClellan's dedication.

Workers lay fresh sod and set up outhouses before the Dedication Day ceremony on April 18, 1939.

Workmen rush to complete construction before the official dedication of the base in April 1939. The guardhouse and firehouse have been completed.

Here is Gate One in April 1938, just before the Dedication Day ceremonies. The heavy rains made the final, hurried preparations difficult for the construction teams and military officers.

Enlisted men leave the barracks at quitting time near Gate One in 1939. Watt Avenue was adjacent to the post barracks area, and many businesses sprung up to cater to the large military population.

Sacramento Air Depot's Dedication Day was on April 29, 1939. The new base was swarmed with dignitaries, aircraft displays, and a very curious and happy public. The long political battle to build the Pacific air depot in Sacramento had been won.

Thousands of automobiles converge at the Sacramento Air Depot Dedication Day on April 29, 1939. This was the first of many traffic jams on Watt Avenue and Roseville Road leading to the base.

Here is a Dedication Day fly-by of a formation of B-18 bombers. Even as its facilities were being completed, the aircraft technology the depot was designed to support was undergoing dramatic changes. The depot would spend the next six decades building and adapting to advancements in aircraft and communications technologies undreamed of in 1939.

Gate Two was the ceremonial entrance to the base that opened directly onto the Headquarters Building and McClellan Mall. The Sacramento Air Depot was officially open.

Two

WORLD WAR II

On December 7, 1941, the Empire of Japan bombed Pearl Harbor, Hawaii, bringing the United States into World War II. In the following days, McClellan Field's military and civilian workers found themselves under great pressure, preparing McClellan's defenses for an anticipated Japanese attack. The all-out national war mobilization brought thousands of new employees to increase McClellan Field's ability to repair planes to get them back to their units. Another urgent mission was training personnel at McClellan Field to support repair facilities in the Pacific. Within a month, the depot hired an additional 2,500 employees.

The first years of the war in the Pacific theater were a period of great uncertainty. The Japanese forces advanced in leaps and bounds, conquering islands with little opposition. Almost immediately, McClellan was operational 24 hours a day to keep up with the demands of a growing war machine. Fear that the United States West Coast would be the next target forced McClellan to operate many nights under blackout conditions.

On March 25, 1942, Col. James Doolittle landed his B-25B Mitchell bomber squadron at McClellan for some quick modifications. Although Colonel Doolittle could not reveal his secret mission, the bombers would eventually carry out the famous Doolittle Raid over Japan. During World War II, McClellan personnel were often asked find solutions to problems they were not originally trained to solve or expected to accomplish. For the remainder of 1942, McClellan would continue finding ways to modify its operations to keep up with the requirements of the Pacific war.

In 1943, McClellan's workload did not ease. During March and May 1943, over 225 aircraft were shipped to the Pacific fleet. The population at McClellan expanded to over 17,500 civilian and 4,200 military personnel. The base infrastructure also grew to accommodate the fast growth of its mission. Aircraft repair facilities, hangars, housing, and support facilities were all built to accommodate the relentless pace of work at McClellan. By 1943, the number of workers topped 22,000. The Allies were gaining victory after victory, and by the end of 1943, their enemies were on the defensive.

In the final stages of the war, McClellan continued to repair thousands of aircraft such as P-38 Lightnings, P-39 Airacobras, P-40 Warhawks, P-51 Mustangs, C-47 Skytrain cargo planes, and B-17 bombers. McClellan was instrumental in supplying, repairing, and modifying aircraft to keep pace with the support demand that was instrumental in America's victory.

Cars jam the Roseville Road the day after Pearl Harbor. Roseville Road was one of the main corridors used to enter McClellan prior to the construction of other entry gates that would ease the pain of traffic jams.

During the war, security at McClellan was a priority. Several gates at McClellan were accessible to the massive inflow of personnel, although traffic jams were commonplace. Seen here is the Gate One entrance, where guards salute an officer exiting McClellan.

McClellan had several fire departments scattered around the air field to respond to distressed aircraft as well as various fires and emergency response calls in and around McClellan Field.

McClellan Field boasted one of the most modern and capable fire departments in Northern California. McClellan fire departments responded to emergencies all around the Sacramento region. Shown here are the firefighters in front of Fire Department One, located just west of Gate One.

Gate Three Guard Shack, located at the Palm Street entrance, was one of the half-dozen gates that were quickly established at the beginning of the war. The Palm Street gate would eventually become the main entrance to McClellan. Of course, a few face-lifts would be conducted to create a presentable main entrance.

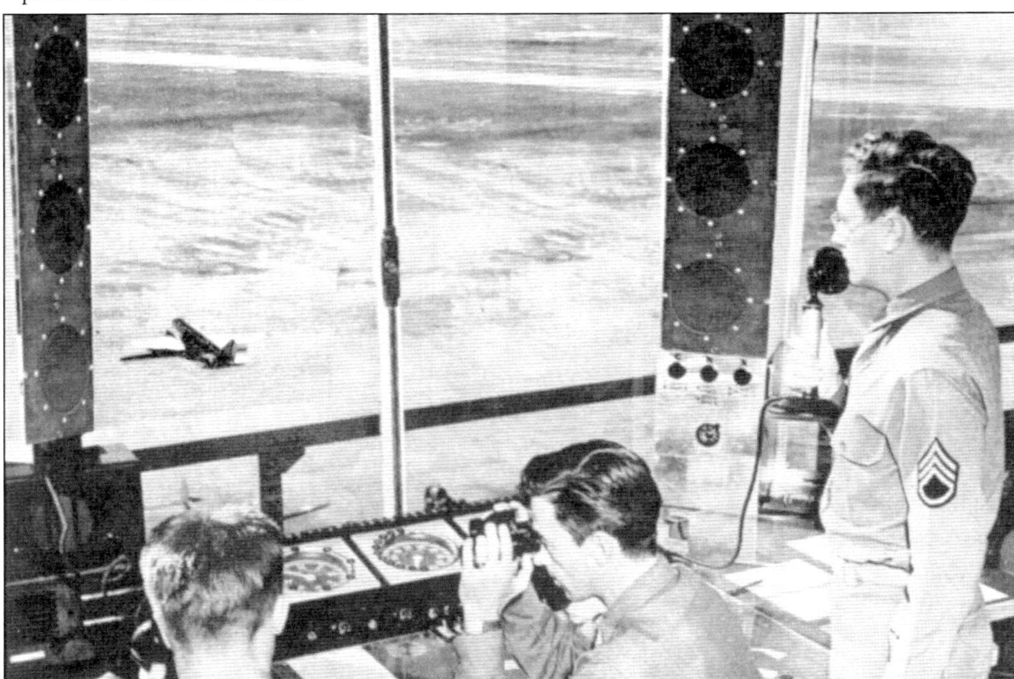

Airfield traffic was controlled from this booth located on top of Building 251. This control room had a broader view of the airfield and was often used to control flight traffic but was also as an outpost to transmit messages to security personnel on the ground.

Although McClellan's borders were closely guarded, an internal element of security was also required. Guards were posted on the flight line to secure the planes so that saboteurs were discouraged from entering the internal security.

The first mass meeting at McClellan occurred at the peak of World War II. General Howard called upon all personnel, civilian and military, of McClellan to discuss the war effort that McClellan would be providing. The military and civilian personnel at McClellan were essentially the pioneers of the base. They would be responsible for expanding the infrastructure of McClellan, increasing their capacity to supply the military with supplies and aircraft throughout World War II.

Many aircraft were staged outside the hangar doors of Building 251. Seen here in the foreground next to a B-29 Superfortress is an early model biplane. The biplane easily fits under the end of the B-29's left wing.

McClellan's airfield was only a few years old when America was pulled into World War II. The taxiways and runways (shown here) would soon be filled with aircraft.

Thousands of military personnel were provided meals three times a day at this chow hall. There were several strategically placed chow halls located at McClellan so personnel would not have to travel far from the work areas.

Feeding the army of workers who crowded into McClellan each day showed the army's ingenuity. When personnel were not near a chow hall, the chow hall would come to them. Seen here is one of many mobile "gut trucks" McClellan used to keep the people fed.

Trainees at McClellan were tested for their aptitudes and levels of proficiency. McClellan's shops were the start of a pipeline of trained technicians who fanned out to every corner of the globe.

Although McClellan was mainly utilized as an Air Force Base for aircraft maintenance and delivery of supplies, there was also a continued need for training. This photograph is of soldiers at the rifle range located adjacent to McClellan east of Watt Avenue.

Cleaning weapons was a common occurrence. Army personnel often cleaned their weapons prior to going to the rifle range as well as coming off the rifle range. McClellan was also used as a conduit for many army personnel shipped to the Pacific theater. Military personnel would train often to ready themselves not only for overseas duty but also to prepare for a Japanese invasion.

McClellan was an army airfield, and soldiers from the base and nearby Camp Kohler practiced combat patrol and security tactics around the facility. Thousands of troops were trained in maintenance and communications at McClellan before being sent on to war zones.

Along with a rifle range, McClellan also had a pistol range. Although it was mostly used by military personnel, civilian personnel were also often encouraged to learn how to operate firearms. This photograph shows a group of women showing their skill of aiming handguns.

Although McClellan's foremost mission during World War II was to repair aircraft, ordnance was also stored at the airfield. Although most planes shipped in and out of McClellan were not armed with ordnance, McClellan stored enough firepower to quell a small invasion if necessary.

Mass physical training of troops was often held at McClellan Field. Former world heavyweight boxing champion Max Bear and his brother Buddy, who had also been a heavyweight contender, were Sacramento natives who enlisted in the Army Air Force and served as physical fitness instructors at McClellan.

Building 251 was constructed with a proactive approach. Strategists determined that the main downfall of the German Air Force during World War I was that they did not have enough repair facilities to counter the Alliance aggression. Building 251 had five separate hangars. This photograph was taken at the beginning of World War II during 1943.

The immense size of the Building 251 hangars was not enough to withstand the workload necessary during World War II. Pictured here is the beginning construction of an additional hangar south of Building 251.

Many requests from all over the Pacific would call this overseas monitoring office at McClellan. Requested equipment and replacement parts were produced at the call center. They would then be distributed to the proper sections to fill those requests.

During World War II, employees would work around the clock in two or three shifts to keep up with repair demand of much-needed aircraft. In this picture, P-39 Airacobras are on the left and P-40 Warhawks on the right.

Military and civilian personnel gather within one of the hangars in Building 251 in front of one of the many airplanes they conducted maintenance on during World War II.

Building 251's main hangars were the cornerstones of McClellan's ability to maintain the required workload during World War II as other hangars were being constructed throughout the war.

Here is a C-47 Skytrain cargo and transport aircraft being repaired in one of McClellan's hangars.

P-38 and P-39 airplanes were maintained and repaired at McClellan. During the 1940s, most of these were worked on in the large Building 251 hangar.

This P-38 Lightning is being overhauled in Building 251 at night. With the threat of invasion looming, hangar doors were often closed so internal lights could be on while all external lights remained off during mandatory blackout conditions.

Here are P-38s at the Sacramento River Docks. Aircraft were loaded onto barges, which made their way down the Sacramento River to the Pacific Ocean.

Roland P. Adams (upper left) trained hundreds of McClellan employees during World War II. Often women gratefully and proficiently filled mechanic duties as their husbands, brothers, and fathers were sent into combat.

During the height of the war, replacement parts were in high demand on the Pacific front. Airplane propellers were carefully crated at McClellan prior to shipment overseas.

Completed in 1938, Building 250 was used for supply distribution for the main repair hangar, Building 251, directly to the west.

Warehouses were quickly but skillfully constructed in order to receive and distribute the massive supplies necessary during World War II. Seen here is one of the many of warehouses that were constructed at McClellan during the war.

Prior to World War II, warehouse construction was not a priority. However, shortly after the beginning of the war, the necessity of warehousing became critical. As shown here, roads in the new industrial area at McClellan were often choked with supplies and materials. This photograph was taken on February 4, 1942.

During World War II, McClellan workers were encouraged to use bicycles for travel around the base as a way of saving rubber and gas. Conservation was essential to preserving resources required to keep the war machine moving.

As the war progressed, McClellan's growing pains were continually felt. Continuous construction of new buildings was necessary to withstand the demand for aircraft repair and supplies. This photograph shows Building 280 under construction in 1944.

The McClellan Mall provided an impressive entry to the base through the VIP gate on Watt Avenue, an inspiring view from the Headquarters Building, and a pleasant town green for the officers' houses. This 1942 postcard celebrates its well-manicured elegance.

Building 3 was the primary medical clinic at McClellan. The clinic would treat both military personnel stationed at McClellan and civil service personnel.

Inspiring patriotic fervor was a key element of maintaining the war effort. Posters, pamphlets, and films reinforcing the importance of every worker's contribution were a staple at McClellan.

After long shifts, military personnel relax at the McClellan post exchange bar. Ration coins were often issued and exchanged for drinks at the bar.

When time allowed, the swimming pool designated for enlisted personnel would be crowded with the personnel and their families during the hot summer days at McClellan.

USO activities were an essential morale booster for the military. Celebrities such as Bing Crosby, Bob Hope, Babe Ruth, and Kat Kaiser visited McClellan to entertain and motivate the workers in support of the all-out war effort. On this day, Bob Hope and Babe Ruth speak to McClellan personnel.

Three

THE COLD WAR

The start of the Korean Conflict in June 1950 put McClellan Air Force Base back on a furious pace of wartime operations. Jet aircraft were rushed through McClellan to replace obsolete propeller-driven fighters. The B-29s still used for strategic bombing became a primary McClellan workload. Trains, planes, and trucks brought supplies through McClellan to the war zone. With this staggering volume of work, the depot ceased being a locally operated repair operation and became a worldwide supply center responsible for all Lockheed and North American aircraft in the U.S. Air Force.

In late 1953, McClellan also became the home base of the 552nd Airborne Early Warning and Control Squadron and their uniquely shaped RC-121 Constellation aircraft. The electronics-laden "Connies" supported many high-priority missions, from monitoring the Nevada nuclear weapons tests to creating the "electronic fence" around Vietnam as part of Operation College Eye.

Perhaps McClellan Air Force Base's greatest contributions to national defense during the cold war were the least visible. The Technical Operations Laboratories of the Air Force Technical Applications Center were among the most sophisticated in the world and provided key information about Russian and Chinese nuclear capabilities. In the 1980s, the Sacramento Air Logistics Center provided support for the highly secret F-117 Nighthawk stealth fighter.

As the U.S. Air Force became increasingly reliant upon technological superiority, McClellan Air Force Base became a national center for the development and maintenance of cutting-edge radar and electronic systems. Radomes, towers, and microwave dishes sprang up from almost every building and parking lot.

The sheer volume of the work done at McClellan from the Korean War through Desert Shield and Desert Storm made the base a vital national-defense resource.

On September 18, 1947, the Army Air Corps was rechristened the U.S. Air Force and became a separate branch of the military services. McClellan Army Air Field became McClellan Air Force Base.

Workers crowd out of Gate One onto Watt Avenue in 1952. McClellan's roads and parking lots strained under the load of post–World War II automobile traffic.

Hundreds of civilians line up to apply for jobs at the McClellan Civilian Personnel Office on the first day of the Korean War. The war boosted McClellan's workforce to 18,000.

The Air Force Technical Applications Center (AFTAC) maintained the Technical Operations Division (TOD) laboratories at McClellan from the late 1940s until 1999. Under a variety of names, TOD monitored foreign tests of nuclear weapons and analyzed fallout and other data collected from those explosions. Aircraft with TOD "Bug-catcher" filters collected dust containing minute amounts of radioactive fallout over the Pacific Ocean and rushed them back to the McClellan laboratories for analysis. The primary TOD labs were Building 628 on the southwest edge of the base near Bell Avenue (1950 to 1988) and the state-of-the-art Russell Building at the far northwest corner of the base (1988 to 1999).

Drained of oil and sealed for storage, thousands of aircraft are parked on a taxiway at McClellan. McClellan was a primary "boneyard" for surplus aircraft returned from the war in the Pacific.

The "front office" of an RC-121 Constellation, including a pilot, copilot, and engineer, prepared for long flights over the Pacific. These "flying radar stations" formed an electric fence around America's borders.

Mothballed aircraft are parked wingtip to wingtip on the taxiways at McClellan. During the years immediately following World War II, more than 650 aircraft of all types were in storage at McClellan, totaling enough fighters and bombers for 13 full air force groups.

A four-engine C-54 Skymaster transport aircraft waits on the McClellan taxiway at dawn for a cross-country flight. The C-54 was the military derivative of the Douglas DC-4, a four-engine, long-range airliner with a three-man crew and accommodations for up to 49 passengers or 26 troops. Originally designed to a specification from United Airlines, the DC-4 had a maximum speed of 274 miles per hour and a range of 3,900 miles.

A parade of F-100 Super Sabres are towed from McClellan Air Force Base to the shipping dock on the Sacramento River. These nose-to-tail "elephant walk" convoys took nearly an hour to make the 10.5-mile trip. The fighters were shipped from Sacramento to bases in the Pacific.

In the mid-1950s, Operation Pull Out was the largest aircraft modification project in air force history. A total of 650 F86-D Sabre jets were torn apart and rebuilt in McClellan's repair shops.

An RC-121 Constellation takes off over a storage yard full of parts ready for shipment. From the start, McClellan Air Force Base served both operational and support missions worldwide.

Here are Boeing B-29 Superfortresses in the maintenance hangar. Every year, more than 350 aircraft were completely overhauled at McClellan.

McClellan was the primary engine repair center for U.S. Air Force aircraft. Three massive concrete buildings for live engine tests dominated the southeast portion of the base. A 240,000-square-foot engine repair facility adjacent to the test buildings specialized in overhaul and repair of every size and type of propeller and jet engine.

"Eve," a B-24 drone aircraft that had been flown through the atomic bomb tests in the Pacific, was flown back to McClellan in 1951 to test the air force's ability to clean and repair engines exposed to radioactivity.

McClellan's maintenance shops modified and repaired U.S. Air Force aircraft from Piper Cubs to Superfortresses.

The Convair B-36 Peacemaker bomber, with its propellers mounted on the rear of its wings, was one of the unique maintenance problems McClellan technicians faced in the first years of intercontinental strategic forces.

The giant XC-99 transport, a cargo version of the B-36 bomber, was the largest cargo aircraft in the U.S. Air Force inventory during the 1950s. Only one XC-99 was built, and the aircraft stopped at McClellan during its test flights. The XC-99 could carry 400 fully equipped troops and 100,000 pounds of cargo on two decks. The wing of the XC-99 was more than 7 feet thick at the root. A person could climb into the wing and work his or her way outboard of the center engine. The 19-foot, square-tipped props were geared to turn approximately one-half engine speed to keep them subsonic, which created an unforgettable throbbing sound. Each aircraft used 336 sparkplugs, most of which required replacing after each mission.

Past and present cross paths on the McClellan taxiway. Here are the F-106 Delta Dart interceptor and P-40 Warhawk waiting for repairs outside of the maintenance hangar. McClellan was the center of F-106 maintenance from 1956 to 1978. During the early 1950s, McClellan engineers and technicians had to simultaneously support the latest jet aircraft fighting in Korea with the Air Defense Command and keep World War II–vintage propeller aircraft in the air.

Every aircraft overhauled at McClellan followed a path from shop to shop as various systems were inspected and replaced. This B-29 waits between Hangars 362 and 365 as it moves through the process.

The uniquely shaped RC-121 Constellation was the most visible representative of McClellan Air Force Base.

Members of the 552nd Airborne Early Warning and Control Wing (AEWC) pass in review. Formal parades and ceremonies were as much a part of an airman's duties as flying missions.

The 552nd AEWC and their uniquely shaped RC-121 Constellation aircraft were the largest flying unit at McClellan from 1953 to 1976.

A 552nd AEWC crew stands for a last inspection before a mission. The RC-121 was a "flying radar station" that could be quickly dispatched to monitor any spot on the globe. The 552nd crews flew long missions and deployed to forward bases frequently, especially during the Vietnam War.

The 55th Air Weather Reconnaissance Squadron (AWRS) operated out of two rows of "temporary" buildings for more than a decade. The AWRS flew daily missions across the Pacific Ocean, requiring extensive mission planning.

As electronic instruments replaced mechanical devices, McClellan's shops became ever more sophisticated. This technician (right) services the guidance compass from a B-29 Superfortress while the specialists test a mobile radar system.

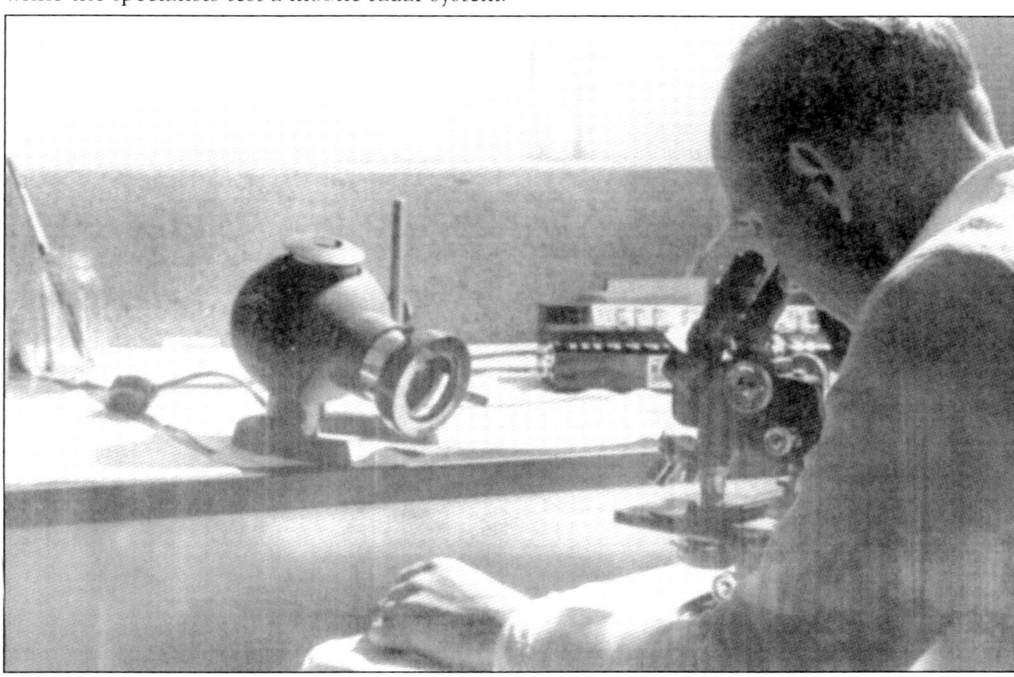

Analytical, quality control, and production process laboratories were scattered across McClellan. Throughout the cold war, McClellan was one of Northern California's premier scientific facilities.

Janette Hickman became the first woman engineer to work at McClellan when she joined the Directorate of Maintenance in 1960. She managed a variety of projects until base closure 38 years later.

Throughout the 1950s and 1960s, the demand for office space far exceeded the supply. Large warehouses and small wooden temporary buildings from World War II were converted into makeshift offices. Finally the need for a new Air Material Center command building became undeniable. Construction of the 350,000-square-foot Austin Building was begun in January 1966 and was ready for its first occupants in May 1967.

Modern dormitories replaced wooden World War II barracks in the early 1950s to accommodate McClellan's rapidly expanding population. Development in the town of North Highlands and along Watt Avenue (visible at the right) boomed during the rapid expansion of McClellan's work force during the cold war.

Millions of tons of supplies and equipment passed in and out McClellan's warehouses and shops every year by train and truck.

At the time of its first flight, the C-74 was the largest landplane to enter production, with a maximum weight of 172,000 pounds (78,000 kilograms). It was able to carry 125 soldiers or 48,150 pounds (21,840 kilograms) of cargo over a range of 3,400 statute miles (5,500 kilometers).

The Boeing B-47 Stratojet jet bomber was a medium-range and -size bomber capable of flying at high subsonic speeds and primarily designed for penetrating the Soviet Union. A major innovation in post–World War II combat jet design, it helped lead to the development of modern jet airliners. While it never saw major combat use, it was the mainstay of U.S. Air Force Strategic Air Command striking power in the 1950s.

Every one of the dozens of intricate instruments on every aircraft were serviced and repaired at McClellan's instrument shops. The meticulous, exacting work kept hundreds of skilled technicians working multiple shifts.

By the early 1960s, McClellan's repair and supply duties demanded ever more sophisticated tools to track and manage its worldwide inventory. Banks of the latest UNIVAC computers began replacing former repair shops and file rooms. McClellan's infrastructure strained under the new technologies requirements for space, electrical supplies, and communications support.

Air shows and aircraft displays at McClellan drew enormous crowds from across the Central Valley. Even at the height of the Vietnam War in 1967, people jammed into McClellan to see the work being done there and to show their support.

Four

LIFE AT MCCLELLAN

While McClellan Air Force Base operated around the clock to service and supply operations all over the world, it was also home to more than 5,000 family members of servicemen and -women assigned there. Homes, churches, schools, stores, recreational facilities, and doctors' offices all coexisted with the runways and repair shops a few hundred feet away. Several generations of children were raised at McClellan in houses with large backyards and playgrounds, while the sound of jet engines ran almost constantly in the background.

Always pressed to keep up with the pace of growth, McClellan's family support services made due with whatever buildings were available. The large concrete building originally designed for the post exchange (which became the base exchange when the Army Air Corps became separate from the Air Force in 1948) was converted to offices to accommodate the rapid expansion of World War II. Old barracks were converted to meet whatever need arose, whether housing a bowling alley, a chapel, or a dance floor for the Noncommissioned Officers Club.

As McClellan's housing slowly modernized and moved out of "Splinter City" and into the Wherry housing area on the main base and the Capehart housing area a few miles up Watt Avenue, life at McClellan centered more and more around families. Shopping, schools, recreation, swimming pools, the hospital, and a movie theater were all within walking distance of the new housing. A military base kept under tight security, McClellan was a safe place for children to ride bicycles, play with their friends, or watch the aircraft take off and land. Former "air force brats" who grew up at McClellan recall climbing in the trees along the fairways of the Lawrence Links Golf Course, getting free cheeseburgers from the clubhouse grill, watching movies for a dollar, and being greeted by name by armed, but smiling, military gate guards.

Inside one of the largest industrial military installations in America lived a close-knit small town.

"Splinter City," a 118-acre community southeast of the main base, was built of temporary wood and tarpaper buildings to accommodate the explosion of soldiers assigned to McClellan in World War II. Splinter City was a complete town, with barracks, a chapel, a post exchange, a swimming pool, a baseball field, a hospital, and a gas station.

More than 1,200 people each day crossed the pedestrian bridge from the barracks and support buildings of Splinter City to the hangars and shops of the main base. The bridge crossed Roseville Road just before the intersection with Watt Avenue.

The Splinter City Theater was built in 1940 and was renovated many times to stay in service through the 1960s.

The Splinter City Theater seated more than 1,000 people. Films cost less than a dollar, and frequent live shows, both professional and locally produced, from Kay Kaiser and his "College of Musical Knowledge" featuring singer Georgia Carroll to the McClellan Follies, entertained the troops and their families.

The "temporary" Splinter City barracks remained in use for more than 30 years. Built from a design that was identical at all World War II army bases, the barracks were wooden structures reinforced with plasterboard and placed on raised concrete foundations.

The Splinter City Chapel was constructed in 1939 and served the spiritual needs of the troops and their families. The original chapel was a standard World War II–era wooden structure with minimal ornamentation, so that it could be flexible enough to accommodate services for any denomination.

After the Wherry housing community was built near the hangars and runway in 1952, a small chapel was built on the main base to serve the residents there.

The new chapel was constructed in 1970 on property north of the base that was obtained in a land swap for most of Splinter City. The new chapel was a permanent, modern structure with custom-designed stained-glass windows and an annex for meetings and social functions.

An honor guard confers final honors on a McClellan serviceman killed in Korea. The funeral, on a rainy day at the Splinter City Chapel, included a three-volley, 21-gun salute.

This photograph depicts a wedding with full honors in 1951. In accordance with tradition, the bride and groom walk under an arch of the raised sabers of the honor guard. It was also traditional, as the couple recess through the arch of swords, that the last two men to make up the arch lower their swords in front of the couple, detaining them momentarily, while the sword bearer on the right gives the bride a gentle swat on the rump with his sword and utters, "Welcome to the air force."

The main installation officers club provided dancing, dining, a well-stocked bar, and a well-appointed environment for squadron functions and after-hours socializing.

The Officers Club pool was one of five pools at McClellan over the years. It was a popular afternoon resting place during the hot summers before air-conditioning.

The officers' mess in Splinter City was a very poor cousin to its more elegant counterpart on the main base.

Officer wives clubs provided camaraderie, social activities, and support for worthy causes. In 1951, these wives organized and modeled in a fashion show for charity. "Coffee Klatches," like the one below, were regular social engagements for officers' wives.

The Noncommissioned Officers (NCO) Club gave sergeants a place to unwind away from both officers and their troops.

The new NCO Club was built on the main base in 1970 as part of the move out of Splinter City. Its large dining room and ballroom made it a choice location for banquets, parties, and wedding receptions. Officers were still allowed in by invitation only.

The Enlisted Men's Club opened during World War II as a place for the junior ranks to unwind with no fear of sergeants or officers.

Through the 1950s and 1960s, the Enlisted Men's Club hosted dances and offered convenient place for airmen to relax without spending their whole paycheck. The club offered an air-conditioned place to cool off and have a drink.

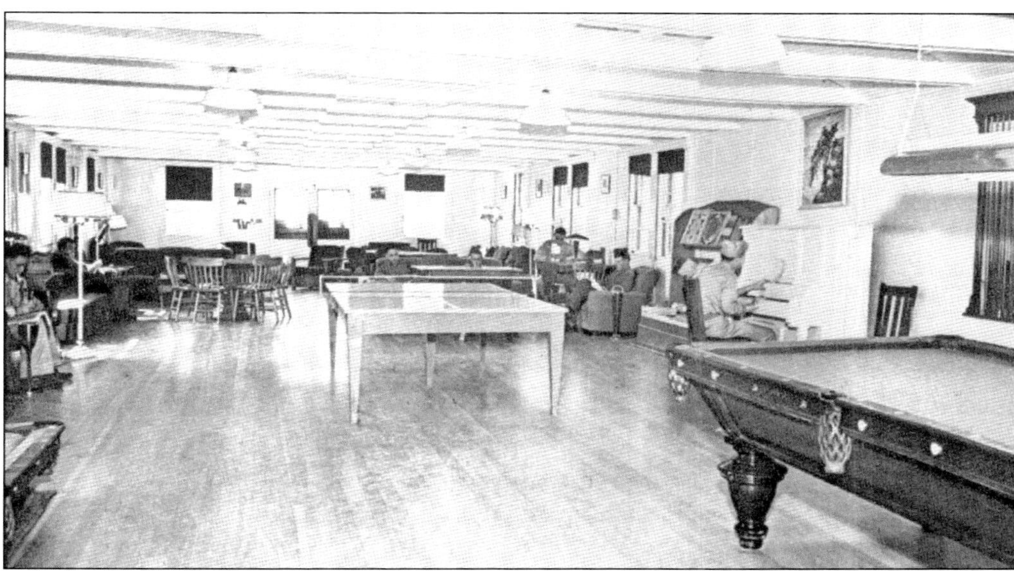

Every company had a day room complete with pianos, pool tables, radios, games, and other ways to pass the time away from duty.

Never as popular as the clubs or sports facilities, the base library offered current newspapers and magazines along with reference materials for the more intellectually inclined. It was also one of the few quiet refuges on the busy base.

The base gymnasium was a large, wooden, barn-like structure built during World War II and barely usable during Sacramento's 100-degree summer weather. A modern, air-conditioned gym was a welcome addition in the 1970s.

McClellan's desirable location made it a magnet for major-league baseball players and minor-league prospects during both World War II and the Korean War. The McClellan team practiced on the base's Winstead Field before large, appreciative crowds of their fellow servicemen and played many games at Sacramento's Solon Stadium. For years, McClellan fielded one of the strongest baseball teams in Northern California.

Fencing was considered a desirable skill for officers into the 1950s. Along with quickening reflexes, it was thought to carry on the martial virtues of chivalry and a more courtly form of battle.

Winstead Field was the center of all outdoor athletic, recreational, and entertainment activities at McClellan. Above, a carnival complete with midway and Ferris wheel covers the field in the 1950s.

The Talbot Fitness Center, built in 1975, covered nearly 30 acres and included a gymnasium, tennis courts, four softball fields, a running track, a miniature golf course, picnic and barbeque pavilion, and an archery court. The track was removed in 2006 and is now the site of the McClellan Air Museum.

Here are members of the 552nd AEWC bowling team. Along with golf and racquetball, bowling enjoyed widespread popularity throughout the military. Every installation sported some manner of lanes, usually including a bar and grill.

McClellan's six-lane bowling center was wedged into a standard one-story World War II utility building.

Expanded in 1970 and refurbished in 1993, the 20-lane McClellan Bowling Center boasted a bar and grill and computerized scoring.

This 1942 postcard shows the main post exchange. The original exchange was located in a large building designed specifically to house it. When World War II broke out, the space proved more valuable for offices, so the exchange was quickly moved into several small, inadequate structures around the base.

When the Army Air Corps became the separate U.S. Air Force in 1947, the post exchange became the base exchange. The McClellan exchange in 1955 sported both signs and set up shop in a former barracks. Floor space for merchandise was at a premium.

For most of McClellan's history, the base commissary was located near the Peacekeeper Gate. The commissary sold groceries at prices below the civilian market and was the preferred food store for military families and retirees still living in the Sacramento area.

Cramped aisles stacked high with groceries were the norm at the commissary. The U.S. Air Force kept grocery prices low for military families, who were typically paid less than civilians, but finding money for new family support facilities were always a challenge.

Refurbished many times, the commissary presented a more modern look in the 1970s, but it was still the same wooden World War II building inside. A fire and the inability to keep up with the heavy customer traffic finally convinced the air force to build a new base exchange and commissary shopping center in 1985.

McClellan civilian employees and military personnel supported a wide range of charities and community services. For many years, McClellan families "adopted" local orphans and treated them to a family Christmas.

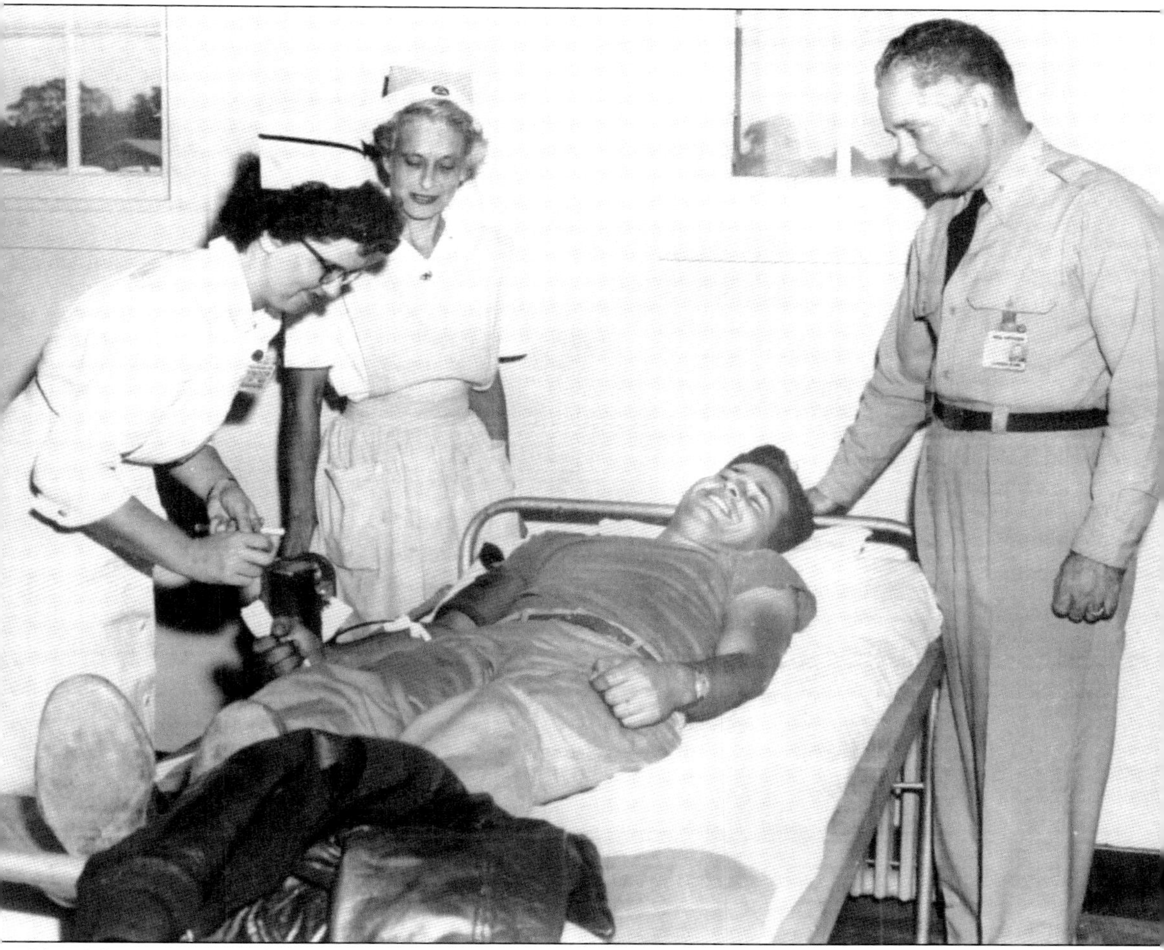

Blood drives were regular events at McClellan, with both military and civilian workers encouraged to give. Many McClellan employees proudly earned membership in the "One Gallon," "Two Gallon," and "Five Gallon" donors clubs.

Like any other town, McClellan had its own corner gas stations. For a time in the 1950s and 1960s, the service included uniformed pump attendants. The Splinter City gas station (below) was demolished in the 1970s. At about the same time, the original base gas station (above) was closed, and a new facility opened across from the new base exchange. The old gas station still exists and has been converted into a locksmith's shop.

In 1952, Capehart housing was built a mile north of McClellan off Watt Avenue. The development provided sorely needed homes for both officers and enlisted peoples' families. The Capehart community boasted its own stores, schools, swimming pool, and gymnasium. The development of modern housing and family facilities at Capehart made it possible for the air force to close Splinter City a few years later and swap the property for land that became the new base recreation center.

Lawrence Links, a nine-hole golf course, was built on land donated by the Lawrence family. Construction of the course was performed by volunteers using Air Force Civil Engineering equipment and took several years. The course officially opened in 1968.

To be a soldier, a person first has to look like a soldier. McClellan's post exchange was where airmen could get a new uniform in just their size. The uniform sales department carried every jacket, boot, wheel cap, insignia, and uniform item an airmen was authorized to wear. Tailors made sure it fit and officers kept a keen eye out for airmen who weren't wearing it just the way the regulations detailed.

Although the new dormitories built in the early 1950s were a big step up from the wooden World War II barracks they replaced, no one would call an airman's life in them luxurious.

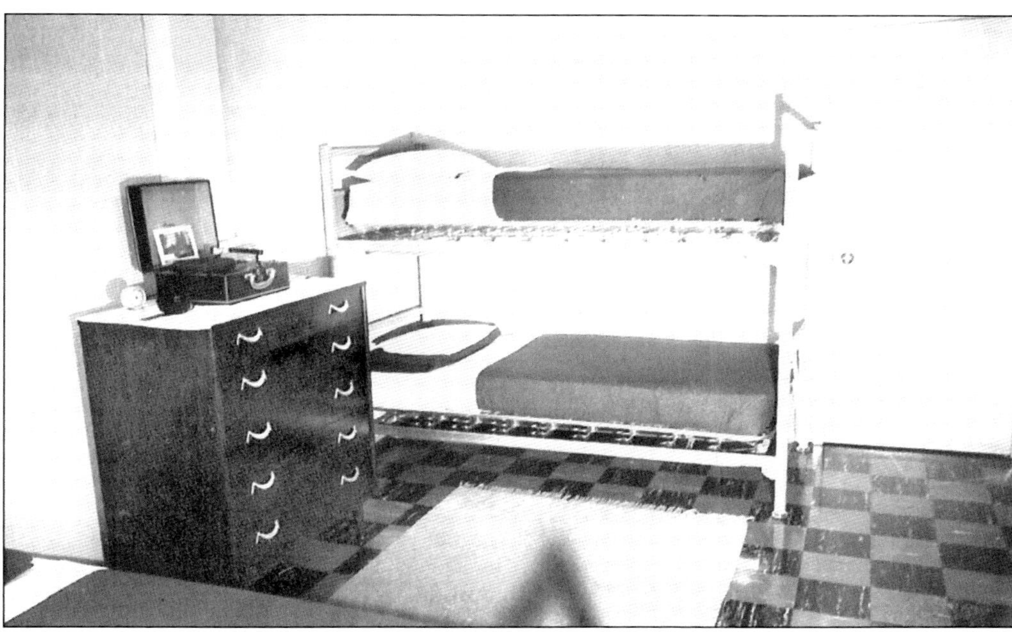

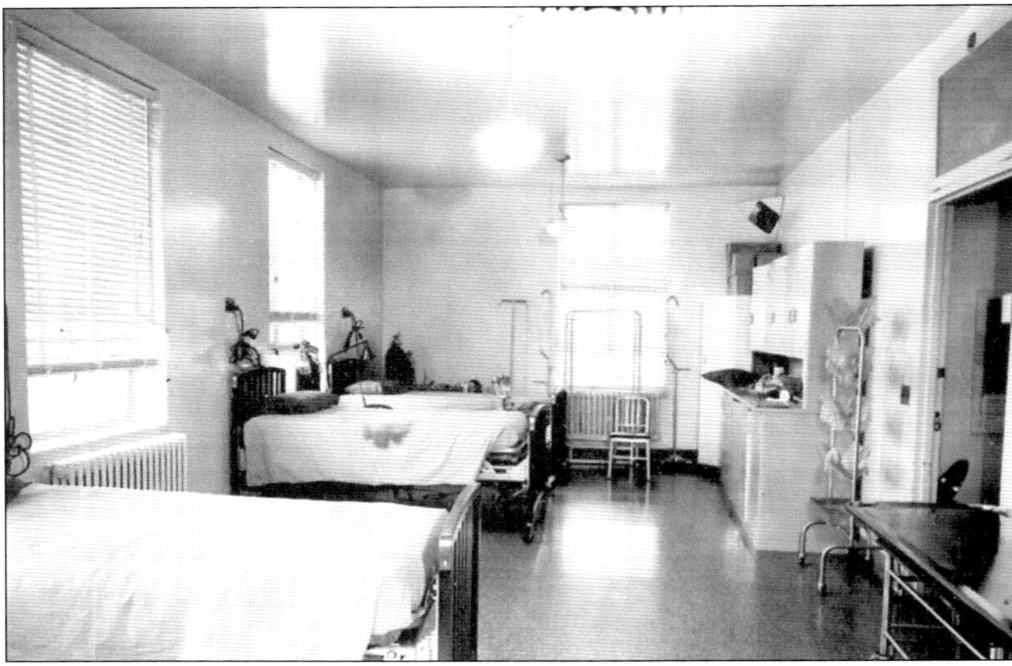

The antiquated and overburdened base hospital, built in 1938, was finally replaced in 1988 with a modern clinic. Operated by the 77th Medical Group, the new clinic included emergency care, pediatrics, optometry, radiology, a full laboratory, and many other services beyond the capabilities of previous medical care facilities at McClellan.

Amidst the constant rush of aircraft, munitions, and supplies, families grew at McClellan. A playground beneath the Capehart Housing water tower waits for neighborhood children to get out of school.

Vietnam brought a crushing workload and the relaxation of many old traditions and restrictions. These airmen skipped the enlisted men's club by building their own patio and barbeque pit behind their dormitory. For more than six decades, people managed to adapt McClellan to meet their needs and make it their home.

After enough barracks were constructed on the main McClellan installation, Splinter City was demolished and returned to civilian ownership. The last building in Splinter City, shown here, was moved to the other side of the railroad tracks. The structure would eventually become a post office and lasted until 2007.

Five

All Good Things . . . McClellan Closes

The heavy workloads and intense pace of the mission at McClellan as it supported Operations Desert Storm and Desert Shield masked the true impact of the end of the cold war. With the collapse of the Warsaw Pact and the Soviet bloc, the need for many U.S. Air Force systems and bases declined dramatically. The air force also faced significant reductions in its budget. The Base Realignment and Closure Commission's (BRAC) rounds of base closures in 1988, 1991, and 1993 closed 22 bases in California and more than 100 nationwide. Each time, Sacramento mounted a vigorous defense of the base, and McClellan survived. But by the 1995 BRAC round, the need to close a depot was unavoidable. Although McClellan was a center of technological excellence, it had no permanent flying units, and California had higher labor and housing costs than other states where bases also faced closure. Despite the best efforts of Sacramento County and the McClellan Defense Task Force volunteers, McClellan Air Force Base and the Sacramento Air Logistics Depot were designated for closure on June 22, 1995. An institution that had defined the entire region for more than 60 years was going away—and taking 13,000 jobs with it.

President Clinton flew into McClellan on July 23, 1996, to give thanks for the hard work and diligence the military and civilian personnel had given patriotically throughout the years of operation. He also personally lamented the loss of "a great place to land Air Force One when I visit Northern California." During this speech, he announced a plan for "Privatization in Place"; a competition between the major aerospace contractors for a wide variety of work being done at McClellan valued at $220 million annually. The Sacramento community mobilized behind this effort, but on September 21, 1998, the air force announced that Hill Air Force Base in Ogden, Utah, and Boeing Aircraft had won the privatization competition. McClellan's role as a U.S. Air Force facility was really ending.

Between early 1999 and the final closure of the base in July 2001, one program after another took their final bows at the Sacramento Air Depot. Support organizations for the F-15 Eagle, F-22 Raptor, F-117 Nighthawk, and F-111 fighter-bomber all made ceremonial shipments of their final orders and decamped to new homes. The last to fly from McClellan was a KC-135 carrying a special package of commemorative flags for departing McClellan employees.

On Memorial Day 1993, President Clinton lands in Air Force One at McClellan Air Force Base.

As President Clinton exits Air Force One, the United States Air Force Band of the Golden West out of Travis Air Force Base welcomes their commander in chief.

With the presidential limousine and the Secret Service entourage close by, President Clinton and Maj. Gen. John F. Phillips walk across the tarmac toward the anxiously waiting and excited McClellan employees.

President Clinton makes last-minute changes to his remarks before addressing the enthusiastic crowd of McClellan employees.

Linda Geissinger of the Sacramento Air Logistics Agency explains to President Clinton how one of the new electric vehicles operates. McClellan's fleet of electrical vehicles was an example of dual-use technology typical of the innovative work performed there.

With the McClellan Color Guard standing tall behind him, the president signs an Armed Forces Day Proclamation. Overseeing the event are Shiela Widnal, Lt. Gen. Dale Thompson, Congressman Vic Fazio, Congressman Robert Matsui, Sen. Barbara Boxer, Sacramento mayor Joe Serna, and Maj. Gen. John F. Phillips, among others.

The all-volunteer McClellan Defense Task Force waged a grassroots campaign to convince the Base Realignment and Closure Commission to keep McClellan Air Force Base open. The task force worked with state and local leaders to promote McClellan's value to the nation's defense.

On June 22, 1995, McClellan Air force Base was officially recommended for closure by the Base Realignment and Closure Commission. This 2001 aerial photograph illustrates how much McClellan Air Force Base had expanded over the years.

On July 13, 2001, official closing ceremonies were conducted at McClellan Air Force Base.

At this ceremony, the symbolic keys to the gates were given to Sacramento County representatives. On July 6, 2001, the flag was lowered by the U.S. Air Force for the last time in front of assembled local and government dignitaries. It was a scene reminiscent of the Pacific Air Depot's Dedication Day 62 years earlier. The flag was then raised again and Sacramento County supervisor Roger Dickenson proudly announced, "Welcome to McClellan Business Park, County of Sacramento."

James C. Barone, chief of the Sacramento Air Logistics Center (ALC), was given the honor of retiring the Sacramento ALC colors. Roger Niello, Sacramento County supervisor Roger Dickinson, Colonel Caudle, Stan Atkinson, and Lieutenant Hutchinson look on.

The McClellan Honor Guard folds the last flag to fly over McClellan Air Force Base during a closing ceremony on the McClellan Mall.

The terrorist attacks of September 11, 2001, struck shortly after McClellan Air Force Base closed. Sacramento County and McClellan Business Park conducted a symbolic remembrance ceremony at McClellan, bringing the community together in a time of uncertainty.

Formerly known as Building 50 before McClellan expanded, Building 250, the former supply headquarters, was constructed in 1938. As can be seen, the facade of the structure has changed little.

Remodeled and modernized, it now houses as the offices of McClellan Business Park. A key milestone in the transition of McClellan into a business park was the selection by Sacramento County of local developer Larry Kelley as the county's development partner for McClellan Business Park. McClellan Business Park's innovative approach to the leasing and reuse of former military facilities produced an unexpected, but entirely welcome, boom in redevelopment at McClellan.

Building 252, a manufacturing and warehouse facility, was remodeled into modern office space for SureWest Communications. McClellan Park's extensive remodeling and rehabilitation of the old air force buildings gave the property new life and a new future.

SureWest rebuilt the communications systems at McClellan Business Park, installing miles of fiber-optic cables to support the computer needs of the new commercial tenants.

First built in 1953, the base water tower on the corner of Dudley Boulevard and Peacekeeper Way was a landmark for incoming planes and visitors. Over the years, the tower was painted with many designs, including a red and white checkerboard and various air force insignia.

The water tower at the corner of Peacekeeper Way and Dudley Boulevard was constructed in 1953.

The Peacekeeper Gate was the main entrance to McClellan Air Force Base for more than 60 years. Security guards manned the entrance and checked every vehicle entering the base, as seen in this photograph from 1952.

With the entrance security posts demolished, McClellan Business Park warmly welcomes tenants, employees, and customers.

As the McClellan Business Park began renovating the former air force base, tenant occupancy began to rise. By the end of 2005, the number of workers employed by commercial businesses at McClellan Business Park exceeded the number of workers employed by McClellan Air Force Base at the time it was selected for closure.